A RIVER OF LOVE

A River of Love

Frederic Ozanam and the
Society of St Vincent de Paul

Michael Casey

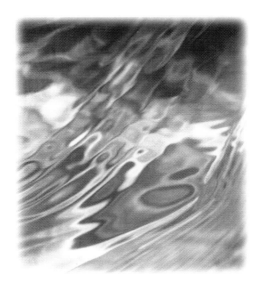

the columba press

First published in 1997 BY
the columba press
55A Spruce Avenue, Stillorgan Industrial Park, Blackrock, Co Dublin

Designed by Bill Bolger
Cover picture by Rita Scannell
Printed in Ireland by Colour Books Ltd, Dublin

ISBN 1 85607 222 3

Acknowledgements:
The publishers gratefully acknowledge the permission of the following for
the use of photographs: Bórd Fáilte for those on pp. 18, 22, 27, 30, 34, 38, 47,
50, 55, 58, 66, 70, 74, 82, 90; Derek Spiers for those on pp. 41, 85; 79, Tony
O'Shea for those on pp. 44, 52, 79; The Society of St Vincent de Paul for
those on pp. 73, 79.

Contents

I would like
to embrace the
whole world in a
Network of
Charity

Frederic Ozanam

Introduction

Friday 22 August 1997 was a very special day for youth. It was World Youth Day. Friday 22 August 1997 was a very special day for Frederic Ozanam. On that day he was put forward as a worldwide model for youth for the third millennium. Friday 22 August 1997 was also a very special day for the Society of St Vincent de Paul. On that day their principal founder, Frederic Ozanam, was beatified by Pope John Paul II.

Who is this Frederic Ozanam? Principal Founder of the St Vincent de Paul Society? Was it not St Vincent de Paul who founded the Society of St Vincent de Paul? No. He is its patron. The St Vincent de Paul Society was founded in 1833 in France by a wonderfully gifted, courageous and idealistic twenty-year-old student called Frederic Ozanam and his young student friends. That's a surprise to many people – even some who know the SVP quite well.

On Friday 22 August 1997 members of the SVP from 132 countries gathered at the Cathedral of Notre Dame in Paris to honour their principal founder. On this special occasion, Frederic Ozanam was introduced to the youth of the world as a young, active, lay Christian with a deep and passionate concern for social justice. To mark this special occasion, the Society in Ireland decided to produce a book which would bring Frederic Ozanam alive for the members of the Society in Ireland and for young people in particular. It was felt that if this young student, with his revolutionary social ideas and great Christian vision, could inspire Popes and challenge governments, as well as found the SVP, then perhaps he could provide challenge and inspiration for the SVP and the Ireland of today, especially its young people.

This is the story, then, of Frederic Ozanam and of the origins and growth of the SVP worldwide. It is also the story of the SVP in Ireland, from its origins during the Famine to its multiplicity of activities and projects today.

This is the story of the SVP, which is also a story of spirituality, a story of lived values in an ever-changing world. It is also, in a sense, a story of Ireland, with its aspirations and challenges, its warts and blackspots, and its contradictions as we approach the beginning of the third millennium.

Frederic Ozanam: Chronology

1813	Born 23 April in Milan of French parents
1815	Moved to Lyons
1829-30	Apprenticeship in Law Office
1831	At 18 wrote defence of the Christian faith
1831	School of Law at University
1832-33	Student leader at the Sorbonne
	Campaign in defence of the faith
1833	Founded SVP
1834	Passed Law Examination
	Petition for 'modern religion' to Archbishop of Paris
1835	Wrote book on 'Two English Chancellors'
1836	Doctorate in Law at 23
1837	Frederic's father died
1838	Wrote thesis on the poet Dante
1839	Doctorate in literature at the Sorbonne
1840	Frederic's mother died
	Professor of Commercial Law at Lyons
	Offered Chair of Philosophy at Orleans
	Offered Chair of Foreign Literature at Lyons
1841	Married Amelie Soulacroix
	Met Pope Gregory XVI
1844	Professor of Foreign Literature at Sorbonne
1846	Met Pope Pius IX re SVP
1847	Wrote book on the Franciscan poets
	Literary History of Italy 8th-13th centuries
1848	Frederic Ozanam goes into politics
	Founder of Newspaper: *New Era*
1853	Died at Marseilles on 8 September, Feast of the Nativity of Our Lady

CHAPTER I

Two dreams

1. A little girl had a dream

A little girl had a dream that there was peace everywhere in the world. All the tanks and all the guns and grenades were burning in a big fire and lambs and lions and children were playing together in a field. And the word 'greed' was taken out of the dictionary and the word 'need' was put in instead. And grown men looked confused and were scratching their heads because children were running the world and women were helping them, and sky sports was banned! And there was a large field called 'God's supermarket' and everyone went in and took enough for their needs, and God was smiling on everyone.

2. A little boy had a dream

A little boy saw all these bodies floating down a river in Africa and he saw little children fishing by the river. The children were shocked when they saw all the bodies and they ran to their mammies screaming, 'There are bodies in the river and they are dead.' And the little boy saw all the men run down to the river and they took the bodies out of the river and said prayers and buried them.

But more bodies kept coming down the river, so the chief called together everyone and said, 'Thanks be to God we have the SVP. I want all the Vincentians or the carers to form a team to look after the bodies and say prayers and bury them.'

And these carers got great status in the village because they looked after the bodies and everyone said they were great and the women dearly liked them because they were so caring.

Then one day the boy in his dream saw a young man – it looked like the chief's son – go up the river, avoiding the bodies as he paddled along. He kept going till there were no more bodies, so he turned back and went up a side river where the bodies came from. He seemed to be there a long time, and then the boy saw him paddling like mad back down the river and running into his father's home shouting, 'I've solved it! I've solved it! The water in the well was poisoned and they didn't know it.'

And so the bodies stopped coming down the river and the chief was very proud of his son for finding the cause of the deaths, but more so for showing initiative by going up the river in the first place.

CHAPTER 2

Where it all began

'The question which is agitating the world today is a social one. It is a struggle between those who have nothing and those who have too much. It is a violent clash of opulence and poverty which is shaking the ground under our feet. Our duty as Christians is to throw ourselves between these two camps in order to accomplish, by love, what justice alone cannot do.'
— *Frederic Ozanam 1840*

Fadó, fadó an exceptional young boy was born in Milan of French parents. He was the son of a man who fought for, and nearly died for, liberty, equality, fraternity. He was a 'war baby' who often heard his father talk with pride of the smallest general with the biggest ego – Napoleon. A boy who would, in time, be able to trace his roots back to the Jewish tribe of Hozannam, which came to the Lyons area of France in the time of Julius Caesar and was converted to Christianity in the seventh century.

A War Baby

On 23 April 1813, Frederic Ozanam, the future principal founder of the svp, was born to Jean-Antoine Ozanam and Marie Nantas, the fifth child of a family of fourteen. Frederic was in fact born in Milan, then under French rule, but when the Austrians captured the city in 1815 Jean-Antoine and Marie moved to their native city of Lyons. Though reasonably well off, the Ozanam family had lost everything through Jean-Antoine signing a Bill of Guarantee for a bankrupt relative.

From an early age Frederic was aware of his father's lack of attachment to money and his great commitment to the poor. His father, a doctor, spent long and late hours among the poor, often for no remuneration, helping them fight the plagues and terrible epidemics of the time. When Jean-Antoine could do nothing to save his patients from death, as was often the case, he opened the little prayer book which he took on all visits, and read prayers of comfort and consolation. Frederic's mother Marie often joined her husband in the care of the sick and suffering poor. Full of faith, the couple always tried to attend funerals together, just to comfort people. As a young child and teenager, Frederic Ozanam would have taken it for granted that parents and adults helped and looked after other people, especially the poor. How could he know otherwise, such was the example of his parents?

These were turbulent times in France. The French Revolution was not long over. Who could forget the reign of terror in '93 and '94? The guillotine struck fear into people's hearts and created many widows and fatherless children. The battles and wars of Napoleon, whose Empire was tottering, and who nearly met his 'Waterloo' in 1815, two years after Frederic's birth, all contributed to making France a very chaotic, very confused and very troubled land. In this short period of its history, France would have three different types of government — an Empire, a Monarchy and a Republic.

And, of course, there was great poverty and social disruption as a result of all the costly wars.

Experience of death

As was noted earlier, Frederic was the fifth child of a family of fourteen. However, out of a family of fourteen, a staggering eleven died. Even from a vantage point of 150 years later, that seems to have been a mortal blow to the Ozanam family. Ten died as babies or very young children, and one, whom Frederic adored, Eliza, died at nineteen years of age. Can you imagine ten cot deaths or the equivalent in one family? Of course, in those days, typhoid and cholera and tuberculosis and other diseases caused much mortality but, nevertheless, the pain of death for so many children must have been awful for the Ozanam family.

It is clear that the experience of death and suffering in Frederic's childhood and formative years had a huge influence on how he valued life and people's dignity and worth later on. Being a war baby, and a pre-penicillin baby, left their mark on Frederic.

Intellectual giant

Frederic Ozanam has been described as an intellectual giant. He had double Doctorates in his twenties, becoming a Doctor of Law at 23 and a Doctor of Literature at the Sorbonne at 26, all with distinction. The man whom Fred's Fashion svp Shops are called after, was a Professor of Commercial Law at Lyons and a Professor of Literature at the Sorbonne! Highly esteemed in academic, church and civil circles, right across the nation, admired as orator, journalist, author, later inspirer of Popes with many of the great social encyclicals influenced by his teaching, this man had a very humble and no-nonsense childhood. In later years, he is said to have thanked God that he had been born into a middle class family, neither rich nor poor, so that he was spared the moral dangers that lie in both the luxury of wealth, and the discouragement of poverty.

Ordinary childhood

Frederic Ozanam seems to have had a fairly ordinary and normal childhood, telling us himself that at the age of eight he was 'headstrong, passionate, and disobedient' (not bad words for a child of eight!). His brother confirms that but adds that he was 'tender to little children and compassionate with every form of suffering'.

Austin Fagan, in his biography of Frederic Ozanam, *Through the Eye of a Needle*, tells us that before they went to full-time schooling, 'their parents had encouraged them, from a very early age, to draw, read, write and especially meet and talk to visitors. Dr Ozanam taught them some Latin while his wife took charge of their religious education.' Fagan continues: 'Frederic was not always

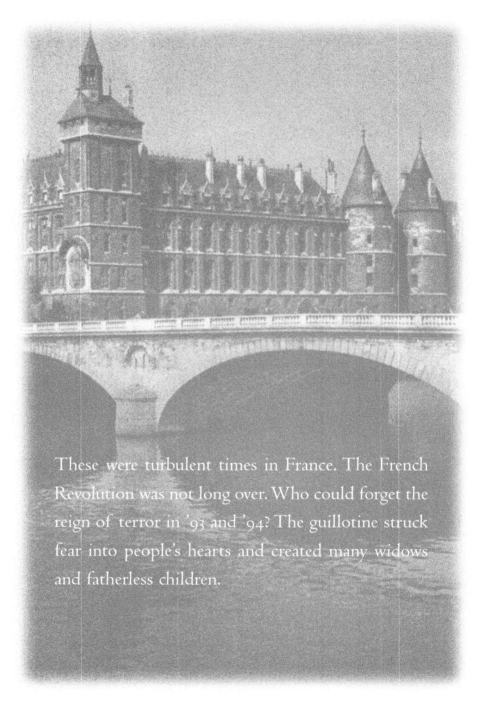

These were turbulent times in France. The French Revolution was not long over. Who could forget the reign of terror in '93 and '94? The guillotine struck fear into people's hearts and created many widows and fatherless children.

a willing pupil. His stubborn moods, tantrums and fits of jealously would often result in his being sent to brood alone in his bedroom' (Fagan, 1989:19). Thank God for normality! Frederic's great consoler in those times was his teenage sister Eliza.

Once Frederic went to school at the Royal College of Lyons at thirteen, he really began to show diligence and exceptional intelligence. He wrote Latin verse and edited a college journal called *The Bee.* At seventeen, when bored in the law office to which his father had sent him, he studied English, German and Hebrew to relieve the monotony! At an early age, we meet a very normal boy with a normal upbringing who was extremely gifted intellectually.

Great heart: Great love

Frederic Ozanam was not just an 'intellect on stilts'. That was very clear in his later life, when he was totally involved with the poor and his beloved or-ganisation, the SVP. At about the age of seventeen, when his father sent Frederic to the law office in Lyons in preparation for being a barrister or judge, his father said, 'He has refined, pure, and noble sentiments and he will make an upright and enlightened judge.' Frederic's upbringing, and his experience of death and suffering all around him, gave him an aware and sensitive heart. Having suffered himself he was capable of suffering with (*co-passio*), being compassionate with others. That is a great gift in life but, of course, it can also be a great cross! The sensitivity, sentiments and compassion of the Sacred Heart seem to have been alive in the heart of Frederic Ozanam from an early age.

Frederic Ozanam's great brain, allied to his sensitive and loving heart, made him special and explains the origins and development of the SVP. If he had a great brain alone he would probably have continued his whole life in the de-fence of truth in the post-revolution and anti-Catholic France at the time — the task that he did so well as a young student from eighteen to twenty years of age. But because he had a great and loving heart, he was moved to action. Hence the SVP.

In other words, Frederic Ozanam didn't just live in his head as so many men do. He followed his feelings too and was all the better person for it. The great conductor, Sir John Barbarolli, once said of a very talented young opera singer: 'She will be truly great when she has suffered.' An SVP conference member in Dublin expressed the same sentiments when he said that being un-employed helped him empathise with all the unemployed people they were serving. 'There's no reality until you have experienced that reality yourself.'

Problems of adolescence

We have seen Frederic Ozanam's experience of poverty and suffering. We have also seen the first signs of great intellectual ability. We have seen some of the circumstances and influences which moulded his young life and later made him what he was. Now, there seems to have been one other 'defining moment' in Frederic's young life. It happened when Frederic was an adolescent, at fif-teen years of age. He began to doubt his faith in God. He says, 'Uncertainty about eternity left me no rest. In despair I grasped at sacred dogma, only to find it crumbling in my hands.' Frederic's world was falling apart — the world that his parents had taught him to trust in above all else. Now that world was in pieces and so was Frederic.

For a whole year, which seemed like a lifetime to Frederic, he struggled and hurt, promising God that he would give his life to the study and promotion of the truth if he got his faith back. This crisis of faith was a crisis of life for Frederic and it shook him to the roots.

As luck would have it, one of Frederic's teachers was the very brilliant philosopher, 'the first philosopher of France', Abbé Noirot. He was also a very gentle and understanding father figure and spiritual guide whom the pupils much respected. It was he, in his wisdom and love, who guided Frederic through the storm into calmer waters. At sixteen, Frederic emerged with a dif-ferent, and probably deeper faith.

A RIVER OF LOVE

Frederic Ozanam: The prophet

And so was born Frederic Ozanam, the great apologist of Christianity and future prophet.

At seventeen years of age, Frederic Ozanam wrote: 'While the young acclaim the glorious Revolution I endeavour to make myself old; I watch, I wait and at the end of ten years I shall say what I think' (Frederic Ozanam, SVP, 1961:5). Not a wild activist here! Here is the historian, the philosopher, the reflector, and seer. Activism would come later in life.

He now set about preparing himself for the mission – like any young person with a dream or a vocation, he didn't do things by half measures. He wrote: 'If I want a book at age twenty-five, I must start my preliminary work at eighteen. I must learn a dozen languages in order to consult original sources and documents. I must study universal history, art and the history of religious creeds in all their depth' (Murphy, 1977:7).

In the meantime, while he was reflecting, and all in his spare time, he wrote a great work in defence of the faith, *Reflections on the Doctrine of St Simon.** This 'defence' appeared in the Paris newspapers and won much praise from leading philosophers, writers and scientists like Lamartine, Chateaubriand, and Ampere, a famous scientist from whom we get the word 'amps' in electricity.

At age eighteen, Frederic had made it onto the national stage, not that he wanted to. Here he was to stay for the next twenty-two years till his death at forty.

For the next two years, at the University of Paris (Sorbonne), Frederic Ozanam would be a leader and inspiration of young people. As an apostle of truth, as a questioner of the status quo in church and state, and as a defender of civil rights, especially of the poor and dispossessed, Frederic Ozanam was giving the prophetic and courageous leadership so lacking and so needed at the time.

He was indeed being a champion of liberty, equality, fraternity at their deepest level. As a youthful seer, idealist and pathfinder, he was linking the

* The St Simon movement was an anti-Catholic movement.

As an apostle of truth, as a questioner of the status

quo in church and state, and as a defender of

civil rights, especially of the poor and

dispossessed, Frederic Ozanam gave

the prophetic and courageous

leadership so lacking

and so needed

at the

time.

macro to the micro, the 'big picture' to the everyday life, history and philosophy and political science to the 'now' reality of the everyday France.

Frederic: A person of faith

At first Frederic was very lonely in Paris. He was also shocked by some of the crudeness of its way of life. He was no different from many a young country boy or girl coming from a fairly sheltered background to the big city. The first psychological shock of leaving the cosy nest of home and the familiar was nearly too much for him, but he was luckier than most as his 'ma and da' had well-off friends in Paris. One of these was M. Ampere who took Frederic into his home for two years, where he felt at home and also met many of the intellectuals of the city.

It was at this time that Frederic wrote: 'I propose to write the literary history of the middle ages – from the fifth to the thirteenth centuries. But in the history of literature I study principally the work of Christianity. All my argument is then directed towards showing how, on the ruins of the Roman Empire, and on the tribes encamped on these ruins, Christianity constructed a new society capable of knowing truth, doing good and realising the beautiful' (Murphy, 1977:6). Note his breadth of vision, allied to his commitment to keeping God and Christianity at the core. He fought for a Christianity that would influence everyday life – help create a peaceful and just society and counteract the upstairs-downstairs mentality of the rich. Frederic's faith was now a great inspiration for him. It illuminated his world and gave impetus to his actions.

He was very like some of the prophets of the Bible – Moses, Isaiah, Jeremiah, John the Baptist – but he was living in France in the 1800s, a time of great change and great confusion. He took risks like the young St Peter and St John, the only teenager among the apostles and the only one of the apostles who went to the foot of the cross with Mary at Calvary. Young people are often braver than adults – 'more naïve,' adults might say, 'and less political.' In that sense they are more 'people of the kingdom', as Jesus said. We adults become fixed in our views, set in our ways like concrete, probably more fearful, and certainly more political.

Getting the church to take risks

As a student leader in the Sorbonne, Frederic was much in the public limelight. He and his other Catholic student friends took on the enemies of Christianity in the academic staff and among other students where necessary. The campus was like a public debating arena where 'persuaders' tried to win students for the different sides. Ozanam, Lallier, Lamache, Tallandier, and others carried on their campaign with vigour, through meetings, debates, leaflets, and the 'media' of the day — the newspapers.

However, in Ozanam's view, there was more needed to fight the forces of the 'secular society' then. The institutional church was not reaching the people, especially the young people. It was too set in its ways and out of touch with everyday life, in their view.

So Ozanam and his good friend Lallier approached the Archbishop of Paris, Monsignor de Quelen, with a petition from the students to have a chair of preaching at Notre Dame Cathedral, 'which in the modern form and in the very scene of daily controversy' would engage the minds and hearts of the people and expound and defend Christianity. They also suggested the most famous and very controversial young priest named Lacondaire. The archbishop heard them attentively, knowing the great work they were doing among students and the public, and promised them that something should be done. Looking over his shoulder at all his own diocesan priests, he had a difficult decision. So he compromised. He appointed seven of the most 'eminent priests' of the diocese to give the sermons. Ozanam was disappointed and dismayed because he knew what would happen. They were preachers of the old school and the world of 1834 was a different world, a 'new continent' as Pope John Paul II would have called it. Talent and skills they had, but their understanding and methods were unsuited to the new needs. Ozanam was right. The experiment was a failure. However, after another visit from the tenacious Frederic, the archbishop was big enough to acknowledge the wisdom of youth and allowed Lacondaire to accept the chair of preaching at Notre Dame. The rest is history. Lacondaire had joined the Dominican Order in Rome and came back to France, where the Order was banned, and ascended the pulpit in the Dominican outfit. Those lectures are held to the present day at Notre Dame.

Ozanam was pleased with his great victory! In his report of the first Sunday, for the Catholic newspaper, *Univers Religieux*, he wrote of an estimated 5,000 people enthralled by Lacondaire's preaching. 'He was the son of our own century. Having renounced its errors he now wished to tell his brothers about the truth which his eyes had seen. We seemed to be witnessing not just the resurrection of Catholicism, but the resurrection through religion of society itself' (Fagan 1989:70).

Birth of the Society

One night, as Frederic and his friends were coming home from a heated debate, they were very angry.

'Who does he think he is?'

'He has some neck!'

'Imagine! The Catholic Church about pie in the sky!'

'Imagine!'

'Show me your works, says he!'

'Probably a thick culchie from Bordeaux or Brittany!'

It bugged Ozanam a lot. There was no intellectual answer to it. Also it was true! But to have to admit it? Didn't the Lord himself say, 'Faith without good works is dead.' Or was it St Paul said it? What does it matter? It's true. What is faith really? An insurance policy? A lovely cosy vision? Lighting candles?

No, it's more than that. It's about building up the kingdom of God on earth. That takes actions. Wasn't that the message of that teenage apostle too – action: 'Because God first loved us, we must love one another.' It's really about

'The question which is agitating the world today is a social one. It is a struggle between those who have nothing and those who have too much. It is a violent clash of opulence and poverty which is shaking the ground under our feet. Our duty as Christians is to throw ourselves between these two camps in order to accomplish, by love, what justice alone cannot do.'

Frederic Ozanam 1840

the equality of all before God. Christ has sent out all his followers to comfort the afflicted and to afflict the comfortable.

That's it. That's a good vision for youth – to comfort the afflicted and to afflict the comfortable. Action is needed.

Show us your works

About this time, Ozanam and his student friends met up with a wonderful elderly Professor of Philosophy called M. Emmanuel Bailly. He became their mentor and father figure. He had been president of a study group called the 'Conference of Literature, History and Philosophy'. When this fell through, he picked up the pieces with Ozanam and others and so the 'Conference on History' began.

It was here, in the spring of 1833 in one of the heated debates, that the famous exchange took place. In response to the 'proof' of Ozanam and friends that the Catholic Church was the one true church, one of the opposition said, 'We agree that at one time your church was a great church and was a great source of good. But what is your church doing now? What is it doing for the poor of Paris? Show us your works and we will believe you.'

After the debate, Ozanam and his friends agreed that perhaps their opponents had a point. Then one of them said, 'Let's visit the poor': and, in a sense, at that moment the svp was born.

Some weeks later, on a bright May evening in 1833, the 'Conference of Charity' was formed under the chairmanship of M. Bailly. Present were Frederic Ozanam, François Lallier, Paul Lamanche, Felix Clave, Augusta La Tallandier and Julius de Voux – six students all in their twenties, all friends of Ozanam and inspired by him.

A tiny stream of love began from that building at 18, Rue de Petit, Bourbon-Saint Sulpice, the headquarters of *Tribune Catholique.*

CHAPTER 3

A tiny stream to a mighty river

I would like to embrace the whole world in a Network of Charity

— Frederic Ozanam

From the time Frederic Ozanam and his young student friends set up the 'Conference of Charity' in Paris (1833), under the paternal guidance of M. Bailly and the patronage of St Vincent de Paul, it has grown from being a tiny stream into a mighty River of Love. If anyone had told these young idealistic and committed students at the time that their little efforts of being with the poor and the elderly would grow into a great worldwide organisation, they would have laughed. Many other groups of students and young people have set up 'social actions groups', 'care of the elderly groups', 'outreach groups', 'youth employment action groups', and they have been happy with the involvement and camaraderie, which is part of the exercise. An added bonus would be if it did a little good for others, especially the less well-off or the needy in society. That is the nature of the young — to be idealistic, to be risk takers, to be involved. The young founders of the 'Conference of Charity' were no different, except perhaps one.

The project of God

Frederic Ozanam probably did not think either that their little initiative would grow and grow and grow. But he did have his eye always on the larger picture, on the macro scene, as well as on the more immediate practical one. In his younger years especially, Frederic thought and talked the bigger picture while he acted on the smaller one with his fellow students. He never let go of the vision and the quest for the plan of God to become a reality on earth. As the nation toppled into ruin around King Louis Philippe in February 1848, and the Revolution broke, Frederic wrote: 'My knowledge of history leads me to the conclusion that democracy is the final stage in the development of political progress, and that God leads the world in that direction' (Derum, 1995:202). While Frederic joined the National Guard to help restore stability, he also set up the new Catholic newspaper, *New Era*, to promote the idea of a Christian democracy in the new Republic.

Frederic's defence of the truth, to which he committed his life at such an early age, was based on the belief that all came from God – creation, the goods of the earth, life, human dignity – and, therefore, all were equal before God. Since all was from God and all his thinking and acting was God-referenced, Frederic saw himself and every Catholic or Christian as a co-worker with God, and as a 'junior partner' in the project of creating a kingdom of peace, justice and love. Even in 1848 when the inevitable, in his eyes, was happening – the revolt of 'those who have nothing against those who have too much' – he still pleaded with responsible French people to 'bring about as general an equality as possible among men; and to make love accomplish what justice and law alone can never do.' Then he added his now well-known teaching: 'Do away with misery, Christianise people (society) and you will make an end of revolutions' (Derum, 1995:204).

Acorns to Oak Trees

Since Frederic saw all the work of charity and the work of justice ('What you do to the least of my brothers, you do it to me') as the work of God, he believed miracles could happen even in the midst of hopelessness. He believed that the creator used 'Miracle Grow' when people did their little bit! Though he and others were in the business of planting acorns, he could always see the possibility of oak trees. And miracles did happen. The Lord has done another 'loaves and fishes' miracle, multiplying the five or six young 'Vincentians' into millions of 'Vincentians' over the years.

Vincentian partnership

With the benefit of hindsight, one can see that God was beginning to weave together a new Vincentian partnership, a winning team! In earlier times Vincent de Paul (1581-1661) and Louise de Marillac had formed a partnership in mission to stand by the side of the poor, the destitute and the marginalised. Their followers, the Vincentian Order and the Daughters of Charity, had carried on that mission in very difficult circumstances but with great courage. Now, nearly two hundred years after Vincent and Louise, the Holy Spirit was stirring in the hearts of a group of young students, and through them, a third partner would be added to the Vincentian team – the members of the svp.

Vincent de Paul as patron

Austin Fagan tells the story of how this came about:

Another newcomer, Leon Le Prevost, made an especially important suggestion during the meeting of 23 April (1833). 'I'd like to ask if the name of a patron saint has ever been chosen for our Conference?' Bailly and Ozanam glanced uncomfortably at one another. 'If no decision has been made, might I suggest St Vincent de Paul?' Seeing no positive reaction, Le Prevost felt some explanation was needed. 'As you know, we've made many contacts with poor families through our good Sister Rosalie. She belongs to the order founded by St Vincent de Paul's own friend.' 'An excellent idea!' exclaimed Ozanam, 'Do we all agree?' Ozanam continued: 'Let's remember, then, that we're choosing a patron for his example and not simply to use some name in a haphazard way. We should regard him as the kind of saint we can try to follow, to imitate. I'd suggest something more. Why not call ourselves the 'Society of St Vincent de Paul?'

It was Ozanam's turn to pause. As in the case of Leon Le Prevost's suggestion, there was complete agreement. The Conference of Charity had its new name: The Society of St Vincent de Paul (Fagan, 1989:58).

He fought for a Christianity
that would influence everyday
life – help create a peaceful
and just society.

Sr Rosalie Rendu

"'Rich Swine!"

The ragged slum-dweller spat out hatred as two young men passed him in the squalid Rue Mouffetard. For their top hats and frock coats identified them, in the Paris of the early 1800s, as of the generally aloof and unfeeling upper classes.

He did not know these two were on their way to bring help to the sick and penniless. Nor that the younger would soon be inviting his Sorbonne fellow students into an organisation that would continuously aid the poor.'

So begins the excellent award-winning book on Frederic Ozanam written by James Patrick Derum. This book, *Apostle in a Top Hat*, gives a most moving account of Sr Rosalie Rendu, superior of a convent of the Daughters of Charity, situated in the poorest area of Paris, a little to the south of the university centre.

Derum continues: 'Whenever Frederic looked, he saw savage and sulky men, many with brutalised features, against a background of ruined houses, many with broken windows, many doorless. As he and his friend Devaux edged their way nervously through the dense mass of human confusion, stepping carefully to avoid the sewage-filled gutter in the middle of the cobblestone pavement, and the foul and fetid rubbish that strewed the street, his heart was sick. He had seen poverty in Lyons, but never had he seen such squalor as in these narrow streets, with their inhabitants packed in the damp, airless, crumbling ruins unfit for cattle' (Derum 1995:52).

Ahead of her time

It was in conditions like these that Sr Rosalie Rendu had worked for thirty years. Being with the poor and loving them were her chief contribution. But she and the Sisters also supplied food, fuel, medicines, and clothing. They also set up nurseries for children of working mothers and ran trade schools, teaching trades to young people to help them break out of the economic bondage of their parents. Frederic and his friends were so much in admiration of Sr Rosalie, and influenced by her love and commitment to the poor, that there is no doubt she was one of the chief architects and moulders of the fledgling SVP.

And so, in those trying and turbulent times in Paris in the 1800s, the foundations for a new and extended Vincentian partnership were laid. Vincent de Paul and the Congregation of the Mission (the Vincentian Order), and Srs Louise and Rosalie Rendu and the Daughters of Charity, would now have a third member in their team, Frederic Ozanam and the SVP. That Vincentian partnership continues the work of its three founders, Vincent, Louise and Frederic, throughout the world today.

SVP worldwide

A year after its foundation in Paris in 1833, the Society began to spread throughout France and later throughout the world. It is now established in 132 countries with almost 1,000,000 members (870,000) and 46,650 conferences. There is a similar pattern to Society work everywhere – to seek out the forgotten and deprived, to offer friendship, love and support to those in need, to be a voice for the voiceless, to work for justice and to empower people. The tiny acorn has become a huge oak tree. In fact, many more acorns have grown on it and taken root in so many, many countries. From the North Pole to the South Pole, from desert to snow-capped mountains and valleys, from the outback to the inner city, from Paris to Panama City, from Belfast to Belgrade, from Kilkenny to Katmandu, from Trim to Timbucktoo, Frederic and his dreamers have wandered.

One could write volumes about the organisation worldwide but, in this book we are concentrating especially on Frederic Ozanam and the SVP in Ireland. This reminds me of the rather eccentric Kerry priest who once wrote a one-volume history of the world. He put the French Revolution in a footnote!

'My knowledge of history leads me to the conclusion that democracy is the final stage in the development of political progress, and that God leads the world in that direction.'

Frederic Ozanam

Origins in Ireland

The SVP was established in Ireland in 1844, in Halston Street Parish near the Four Courts, Dublin, just eleven years after its foundation in Paris. It was brought to Ireland by Dr Woodlock, President of All Hallows, later Rector of Newman's Catholic University. Dr Woodlock presided at the first meeting at the White Cross Rooms, Charles Street West, on 14 December 1844, until the Conference appointed a layman, Redmond Peter O'Carroll, as its first president. O'Carroll would, unfortunately, die of typhus three years later. Dr Woodlock became Spiritual Director and held this post for thirty-four years till he was made Bishop of Ardagh and Clonmacnoise in 1879. There were nineteen members at the first conference, of whom six were lawyers and three were doctors. Those present included John O'Connell MP, son of Daniel O'Connell the Liberator, and John O'Hagan, an active member of the Young Ireland Movement and later the first judge of the Land Commission Court. He is supposed to have written the first annual report. Like his friend the poet, Denis McCarthy, who was also a 'Vincentian', O'Hagan was appointed Professor of Political Economy at the Catholic University, later UCD, with McCarthy appointed as Professor of English Literature. Young men following in the footsteps of Frederic Ozanam! O'Hagan, McCarthy, and their friend Richard Dalton Williams, who was also a 'Vincentian' and poet, were young radicals and rebels who wrote and worked for the good of Ireland and the poor.

Denounced as a secret society

In those early years, young students and rebels were attracted to the SVP because they saw it as an organisation which helped the downtrodden. Another young rebel, Kevin Doherty, was convicted of treason and transported to Van Diemans Land, Australia, as was John Sarsfield Casey ('the Galtee Boy'), the first secretary of the Mitchelstown conference. O'Hagan is reputed to have written an article in *The Rambler* criticising some Protestant journals in Dublin which had described the SVP as a 'secret society'.

The Famine

In an article in the *Bulletin* (Autumn 1996), Gerry Martin, svp International Vice President, quotes from dockets of the Society dated 16 January 1847:

'The Annals of our Society can furnish few instances of greater misery than this. Friendless, landless, penniless, without food, without health, without hope, the wretched family, sick and shivering, starves in a corner, while their father is vainly looking for employment and the miserable, half-clad mother – herself requiring at least repose, for she is pregnant – is daily less and less able to oppose the strength of maternal instincts to the onset of disease. Besides the fullest allowance of bread, meal and soup, we think the Society might reasonably advance some money to redeem pledged clothes and pay the rent (one shilling a week) for those utterly destitute outcasts.'

The ravages of the Famine numbed the whole country and decimated the population. One hundred years later, its effects must be still affecting us as a people, but we have always been in 'denial' about it.

When the Famine was at its worst in 1847, there were still only ten conferences in Ireland, but in common with other relief organisations they threw themselves into the task of relieving the suffering of those who lived or died.

To aid the infant Irish Society, the Council General in Paris held an appeal and sent £6,000 and the French Hierarchy sent £15,000. Years later in 1868, 1871 and 1875, when the French had hunger and disaster in some of their provinces, the Irish conferences held collections and so returned the generosity of the French.

The Society grows

The Society extended to Cork and Waterford in 1846, Limerick in 1847, and 1847 also saw the setting up of a conference in Kilrush, the first small town in Ireland to join the Society. Kilkenny got a conference in 1848 and Connacht had its first conference in 1849 when one was set up in Galway. The svp 'Network of Charity' extended to the north of Ireland in 1850 with the setting up of conferences in Drogheda, Newry and Belfast. It is of interest to note that the first secretary of Newry was a young solicitor named Charles Russell who later became Lord Chancellor of England, the first Catholic to hold the position since the Reformation.

In those early years, poverty and distress were so widespread and all-pervasive, that the conferences were almost totally taken up with giving material help. But as time went by the Society began to expand, both in terms of locations and activities. For instance, it was suggested to the conferences in the Society's Report of 1846 that they should establish lending libraries, set up depositories of old clothing, devote themselves to improving the housing conditions of the poor, and assume patronage of children and apprentices.

The Bulletin

It took a few years before innovations began to emerge. The first of these came from Belfast. Some very creative members of the barely two-year-old Conference of the Virgin Mary in Belfast, suggested that it would be most helpful to the conferences in Ireland if some of the contents of the *Bulletin* in Paris, concerning Society happenings around the world, were translated and put in an Irish *Bulletin*. The conference itself did just that and so the first *Bulletin* saw the light of day in Belfast in 1852. In 1856 the first orphanage was opened in Mount Brown, Kilmainham, Dublin. Prior to 1900 there was no college conference and no junior conference in Ireland. By 1919 there were 258 conferences (56 in Dublin). Hostels for the homeless and holiday homes (Sunshine House, Balbriggan, 1935) were opened; Ozanam House on Dublin's northside and Myra House, Francis Street on the southside, were set up as central meeting places.

By 1945 the number of conferences had doubled to 485, many young people were joining, and the Society was becoming much better known by the public.

Today there are 1,000 conferences, with almost 11,000 members in thirty-two counties.

'Do away
with misery,
Christianise
people and
you will make
an end of
revolutions.'

Frederic Ozanam

A RIVER OF LOVE

A brush with the Divine

Frederic Ozanam loved images, as we know from his interest in art and literature and also from some of the beautiful images he used in his lectures and writings. For example, he spoke of building 'A worldwide network of charity'; he also said, 'We are all like tapestry-makers, only able to see the back of the work, with no idea of the beauty of the front until it is revealed to us, maybe in heaven.' Frederic can now, with God, see the beautiful tapestry of the worldwide work of the SVP. And what joy he and his co-founders must take in that!

So also must the Irish tapestry or patchwork quilt of the SVP's projects and works in Ireland, be a beautiful work of art, stretching all the way back to the Famine. Like many of the patchwork quilts designed today by community groups in Ireland and worldwide, especially those dealing with women's issues, poverty and aids, the SVP tapestry or patchwork quilt would reveal a lot of suffering and sadness, inequality and injustice, as well as new beginnings, new hopes, new love. Like any great work of art, darkness and light coalesce and highlight each other. This 'picture of Ireland', painted by the SVP in over 100 years of service, would also reveal touches of the 'Master's Hand'.

CHAPTER 4

A spirituality for today

*Mr Business went to Mass and never missed a Sunday
but Mr Business went to hell for what he did on Monday!*

This chapter is about the 'internal environment' of the SVP, its 'soul' or 'life blood'. The SVP is a 'value-driven' or spiritual organisation, not a profit-driven or politically-driven organisation. The little rhyme above, a relic of the fire and brimstone Redemptorist preachers of the past, is about the relationship of religion to everyday life – or the lack of relationship. Religion or spirituality mean nothing if they are not lived. Spirituality is about the living of beliefs in everyday life, about applying beliefs about God and the values of God (morality), to everyday life. Spirituality is expressed in right relationships with God and with each other. For Christians, Christ is the great model of that spirituality or way of life.

Frank Sheed, a great speaker on Christianity at Hyde Park in London for many years, tells a story of being interrupted one day by a rather unkempt young man from the crowd. He shouted 'Your church has been around for two thousand years and look at the state of the world!' Sheed answered back, 'Water has been around for two million years and look at the state of your neck!'

Sheed said he didn't mean to hurt the young man's feelings but couldn't resist the temptation to make a point. It was all part of the cut and thrust of public debate, as Frederic Ozanam found out one hundred years earlier in Paris.

It was in answer to the same type of challenge, 'What is your church really doing about poverty?' and 'Show us your works, and then we'll believe', that Frederic was pushed and inspired to set up the SVP. The call and the challenge is for every person to live their spirituality. Full human development is achieved through the growth of the spirit of each person in relation to God and others.

Christ and spirituality

'What is the greatest commandment?' he was asked. 'You shall love the Lord your God with all your heart and all your soul and you shall love your neighbour as yourself.' These were some of the greatest words ever spoken. These two little exhortations, two sides of the one coin, summarise the core teaching of Christian spirituality. They are a summary of the ten command-ments, the beatitudes and all the teaching of the two testaments of the Bible. All the rest of Christ's teaching was commentary and footnotes on this great text. In like manner, all the different spiritualities of all the Christian churches and founders of Religious Orders are merely different expressions of that core Christian spirituality. Some emphasise the mystic or contemplative side of Christian spirituality, like monastic or contemplative or 'desert' orders, while others emphasise the prophetic, justice and 'action for the kingdom' side of the message. Jesus lived both aspects and many people and groups have tried to do the same.

Christ has given, in two lines, the recipe for human happiness at both the individual and communal level. St Vincent de Paul, Frederic Ozanam and many others have tried to expound that core of Christian spirituality and live it themselves. The SVP, as a Christian organisation, must first and foremost model itself on the teaching, the values and the practice of Jesus. Frederic Ozanam never ceased to do so in his own private life, in his immediate rela-tionships with family and friends, but most of all in his prophetic crusade for Christian liberty, equality and fraternity. He continuously proclaimed that Christian conversion was the greatest revolution of all.

A value-driven organisation

As I was doing research on the SVP in Ireland, I asked a senior civil servant,

'Justice is a fixed star which human societies
try to follow from their uncertain orbits.
It can be seen from different
points of view, but justice
itself remains
unchanged.'

Frederic Ozanam

who is an expert on strategic planning, to give me his views on the organisation and where it was going. His answer surprised me: 'The St Vincent de Paul Society, that's a value-driven organisation.' That was the core for him.

He didn't say, 'that's an organisation that works with the poor', or 'that's a voluntary organisation', or 'that's a much respected organisation in Ireland', or even 'that's a male, middle-class group of do-gooders'. He said, 'that's a value-driven organisation.' That's an organisation of people who joined because they felt called deep down to work for God, and to work for the poor, to work for justice and equality and to make a better world. The SVP, in other words, is an expression of spirituality.

SVP spirituality

'When I give bread to the poor, they call me a saint. When I ask why the poor are hungry, they call me a communist.'
– Bishop Helder Camara

When one is writing on spirituality for members of the SVP, one is aware of the futility of trying to make the Pope more Catholic! So many are dedicated Catholics, faithful to their God and their church, and have lived out their religion/spirituality through the SVP especially. But every Catholic and every SVP member is called to more, to conversion, to be more aware of the call of Christ today, especially to move from 'saving our souls' (or private salvation) to a spirituality of service and of justice. It is very important to include the communal and social aspects of the faith as Christ always did. This has not always been our greatest strength in Ireland nor is it today. Why is Irish society, which has been almost totally Christian, so unequal ?

Isn't it a totally Christian Ireland that has given us the Ireland of today — the Ireland of huge inequality, the Ireland of multiple splits, north and south, rich and poor, employed and unemployed? In other words, all of us Christians haven't applied our Christianity enough to how society is run in Ireland. The pre-Vatican II Catholic Church in Ireland put more emphasis on personal salvation than it did on the communal aspect of our religion. Vatican II restored the balance of the personal and the communal aspects of Christianity, but its teachings have often been ignored or not put into practice.

Bishop Helder Camara's comment above is one which reflects the clash of the two spiritualities. 'When I give bread to the poor, they call me a saint.' 'They' are the well-off. 'You are a saint. You are doing great work, I could never do it', they say. They want to see the poor helped. But they don't want justice and equality for the poor.

'When I ask why are the poor hungry, they call me a communist,' says Camara. 'They' again are the better off, the non-poor. Why the huge change of attitude? Why do the better-off members of society want to help the poor but not want justice and equality for the poor? Why are they comfortable with the privatisation of religion and spirituality but uncomfortable with a spirituality of justice and equality? Remember Frederic's words to his brother Alphonse who was a parish priest in Lille? 'If a greater number of well-educated (i.e. well off) Christians and especially churchmen had shown some concern for the poorer classes, we could feel happier about the future' (Fagan, 1989:124). He also said to priests, 'You will be called communists (if you organise working-class movements) just like St Bernard was called a fanatic and a madman' (Fagan, 1989:188).

I will now explore the relationship between personal spirituality and a spirituality of justice, because this question of spirituality has vital implications for the svp as an organisation, as well as for each of its members.

A. Personal spirituality

From a close reading of the svp literatue, it would seem that the svp has a strong 'spirituality of the personal'. This is about developing one's own spiritual life through the work, and also treating people with respect. One sees a great emphasis on personal spirituality in the literature of the svp over the past forty years. This spirituality emphasised personal salvation and achieving

Why is Irish
society, which
has been almost
totally Christian,
so unequal ?

salvation through service of the poor. Critics of the SVP said this spirituality was going to heaven on the backs of the poor. Much emphasis in recent years has been placed on respect for the poor. 'Do I see the Sacred in each person I visit?' is a Conference member's expression of this personal spirituality. The development of this personal spirituality must be ongoing in the SVP in order to nurture the members' own spiritual lives. Much of the very dedicated work of the SVP in Ireland is a product of this personal commitment to Jesus. But the needs of the marginalised need something more. They need a spirituality of justice.

B. A spirituality of justice

A spirituality of justice is based on an attitude that puts need before greed, right before might, and justice before 'charity'. Justice for all, a just society, equality of all before God, are its goals. Nobody likes having to accept charity.

Nobody worked harder than Frederic Ozanam for justice. Justice was the underpinning of all his lectures on law. In his inaugural lecture on Commercial Law in 1839, he stated his case: 'Justice is a fixed star which human societies try to follow from their uncertain orbits. It can be seen from different points of view, but justice itself remains unchanged' (Fagan, 1989:199).

Suggesting things like a minimum wage, the idea of a Christian Democrat Society (seen by many of his supporters then as communism), and equality for all, show Frederic Ozanam to be a far-seeing prophet, a long way ahead of his time.

Frederic always put Jesus up as the great model of justice – Jesus, the greatest of the prophets, who gave his life trying to bring the justice of God alive in this world. Edward Schillebeeckx OP, one of the architects of Vatican II, said if there was one word to describe the mission of Jesus it would be 'equality'.

For Jesus, love was his meaning and equality was his mission. The great biblical test of the Last Judgement, by which the value of all our lives will be judged, is a practical expression of this central egalitarian mission: 'Come ye

Blessed of my Father ... for I was hungry and you gave me to eat, I was thirsty and you gave me to drink, I was naked and you clothed me ... I was in prison and you visited me.'

If the primary goal of Jesus' mission on earth was equality, then the central mission of the SVP must be one of equality.

SVP and justice

Jesus never accepted an upstairs-downstairs society. Jesus never accepted a two-tier society. Nor can the SVP accept it. But if the SVP is to have a true spirituality of justice, its members must look at themselves too as individuals and as a society. All of us need a change of heart. If there is a two-tier society in Ireland, and there is, then most members of the SVP are in the upper tier. The members of the SVP are part of the problem as well as part of the solution. So also are members of all the churches in Ireland, members of government, of the Civil Service, the Gardaí, all the professions, the bigger farmers, the business community. All are part of the problem. All the decision-makers come from this tier too. That is why the SVP as an organisation is called to and is, in many ways, trying to fulfil this difficult, prophetic role in Irish society. Being, for the most part, from the side of the 'haves' and the better-off, it is trying to make an option for the 'have nots', an option for the poor. This is not easy – Jesus never said it would be. But it is a great mission.

It was certainly the mission of Frederic Ozanam all his life. He, in his life, tried to marry his own personal spirituality to a spirituality of service and a spirituality of justice. The SVP must try to model its work and spirituality on that of its principal founder. That is a very great and very difficult challenge for each member of the SVP and for the whole organisation. Frederic expressed this challenging and prophetic spirituality to his own brother Fr Alphonse when he said: 'Parish priests must give up their little comfortable parishes, their flocks which are highly selective but still surrounded by a teeming population which they do not know. They (parish priests) must turn towards those

'It is truth which will always rise up to judge political systems.'

Frederic Ozanam, 1831

who have nothing' (Fagan, 1989:204). I'm sure Fr Alphonse must have loved his little brother for that advice!

Community or apartheid

A spirituality of justice says, with Gandhi, that 'there is enough in the world for everyone's need but not enough for everyone's greed.' It says, with Trócaire, that we must 'live simply so that others may simply live'. It says that no man or woman is an island. It says that poverty is structural and social as well as individual. It says that people create poverty and 'sinful social structures'. It says that people also create marginalisation and marginalised zones and divisions. God never created division in his family, by colour, creed, race or place. God only created community. Apartheid came from people's hearts and prejudices. A spirituality of justice tries to have equal relationships in all situations, not 'win-lose' or 'power-over' relationships. Above all it tries to build community rather than division.

Bill Cleary, in his speech when retiring as President, after a very wide experience of the svp and the Ireland of today, put his finger on exactly this issue. Bill put it positively when he said, 'The key to the future is having and building loving caring local communities.' So a bedrock principle of spirituality and people's sense of well-being is community. It was also the key shift of Vatican II in its understanding of itself as church – the shift from seeing itself as an institution to seeing itself as *communio*, as a community of people, all equal, all full members of God's family.

Christianity as creed (beliefs) and Christianity as institution (structures) does not fulfil the spiritual or social needs of people today, especially in urban settings. Only Christianity as *communio*, as a living, caring, egalitarian community, can do that. The basic task of the church today and the basic task of the svp as a Christian lay organisation is not just to help people individually but to build caring communities.

Nothing is outside spirituality

Spirituality, and especially a spirituality of justice, beams its light on every aspect of life and society. Every decision — political, economic, social — enhances or devalues the soul of a nation and the spirit and life of its people. Probably the most important moral decision for any nation's well-being is the annual budget. It is, above all, about justice, equity, community care, access to basic needs — or marginalisation. All economics is about morality and people's social well-being, or the opposite. One could say that the science of economics is bankrupt if it hasn't a moral base. The free market without social concern is dangerous and destructive.

Nobody reminded us more than Frederic Ozanam that politics is about spirituality and must be based on the gospel. Ozanam wrote volumes on this topic. In a lecture on Dante in 1848, he wrote: 'You have always known me passionately devoted to liberty and to national prosperity, to the kind of reforms (of political structures) which encourage moral and better lives, to the proclamation of equality and fraternity (solidarity) which are simply a fulfilment of the gospel in our temporal world' (Fagan, 1989:200).

Again he wrote, in May 1831, as an eighteen-year-old: 'It is truth which will always rise up to judge political systems' (Fagan, 1989:201).

As somebody said recently in Ireland, 'If religion or spirituality had nothing to do with politics, Jesus would not have been crucified' (*Spirituality*, May/June 1997:162).

The challenge today for the svp, as a value-driven organisation and an organisation for social justice, is to clarify, deepen and broaden its spirituality.

Linking faith and everyday life

I want to explore, in this section, the relationship of faith to everyday life. The living of faith in everyday life is spirituality. That is the arena in which the battle between good and evil, light and darkness, equality and inequality, poverty and riches, is being fought in Ireland and worldwide today. That is the

> Make love accomplish what justice and law alone
> can never do.
>
> *Frederic Ozanam*

arena where every member of the svp, and every member of Irish society, is making moral decisions everyday. That is the arena in which battles will be won and lost for equality, for justice, for the poor, for the good of Irish society in general.

Frederic Ozanam said as much about faith and the battles of everyday life in French society. On 13 December 1836 he said: 'Our duty as Christians is to place ourselves between two irreconcilable enemies. It remains to be seen which will win: the spirit of selfishness or the spirit of sacrifice' (Fagan, 1989: 208).

Philip Murnion SJ makes an interesting point about this link between faith and life, or the lack of it. He says:

'Profession of faith is not the same as living the faith. It takes spirituality to turn the profession of faith. And spirituality is our challenge' (Casey, 1992:136).

Spirituality versus secularity is a basic issue for the churches and the svp today. As Murnion says: 'There is a seriously growing gap between faith and life. I'm talking, of course, about the process of secularisation. For secularisation does not mean specifically loss of faith, but the isolation of faith and religion from the rest of life' (ibid).

A sense of the Divine

We have different names for the multitude of different ways to God. Just as no two people have the same fingerprints or footprints, no two people have ever gone exactly the same way to God. Each of us is unique, has a unique relationship with God, and therefore treads a different path to God from anyone else.

We speak of 'Christian spirituality', 'Eastern spirituality', 'Creation-centred spirituality', 'Celtic spirituality', 'Vincentian spirituality', all the ways that the founders of Religious Orders prayed or related to God and invited their followers to do the same. 'Franciscan spirituality' is another one of these – the rich young man leaving all behind to live in total poverty for the sake of the kingdom, to get rid of the baggage and live close to God.

All through the centuries people have been 'value-driven' and spiritually driven. They have been driven to honour God or the gods, Sun Gods, Mythical Gods, Gods on Holy Mountains like Mt Olympus, Mt Fuji, Croagh Patrick. From the beginning, humanity has been spiritual – driven to worship of God and service of each other for God.

The core of spirituality is that God is the ground of all our being. God is our Creator, our heartbeat, our oxygen tent, our source of life, and the energy in the universe. As the Bible says, God is the 'alpha and the omega', the beginning and the end of all things.

This reality has been expressed by billions of people since time began. Through all the major world religions, through thousands of Religious Orders, in deserts, in monasteries, God has been honoured and served; through many spiritualities – mystical, prophetic, contemplative, creation-centred, sacramental, action-orientated, clerical and lay – God has been served; through the spiritualities of all the native peoples of the world, through their rites of passage at different stages of life, through their naming of the different seasons in honour of God and having blessings for almost every occasion, God is honoured and spirituality is expressed.

James Joyce portrays young Stephen Dedalus thinking about God:

'God was God's name just as his name was Stephen. Dieu was the French for God and that was God's name too; and when anyone prayed to God and said Dieu then God knew at once that it was a French person that was praying. But though there were different names for God in all the different languages in the world and God understood what all the people who prayed said in their different languages, still God remained always the same God and God's real name was God' (Joyce, 1916:16).

All people are expressing their spirituality in their own different ways when they decide to honour God or help other people. The svp member visiting the elderly psychiatric patient, or the member visiting a poor family in inner city Belfast on a night of driving snow, are expressing their spirituality. So is the

'Secularisation does not mean specifically loss of faith,
but the isolation of faith and religion from
the rest of life.'

Philip Murnion SJ

young third-level student visiting Louth Derg or the elderly Sligo farmer climbing Croagh Patrick for the thirtieth time, or the young single parent bringing up her child. Religions and religious acts, and the living of beliefs, are all expressions of spirituality.

All of Frederic Ozanam's life was an expression of spirituality in this linking of faith and everyday life. Even in presenting himself for election to the National Assembly in May 1948, which he did reluctantly on the persuasion of friends, he made that connection between Christianity and the world. In his election manifesto he wrote: 'To this end I have always brought a passionate love for my country, zealous support for working-class needs, and a life-long aim of linking Christianity and life' (Fagan, 1989:160). As a matter of interest, Frederic, though he lost the election, got 16,000 votes after only a two-week campaign!

So much in common

In a famous book on the history of religions, the great scholar Heiler listed seven principal areas of unity to be discerned in all the major religions of mankind: Christianity, Judaism, Islam, Zoroastrian Mazdaism, Hinduism, Buddhism, Taoism. The following is a summary of these areas of unity as he discussed them

1. People have always believed in the Divine, the Other, 'God'.

2. People have believed that the divine, while transcendent, is also immanent in human hearts and in our world. We are 'temples of the Holy Spirit' (St Paul); God is nearer than our very pulse (The Koran).

3. This transcendent reality is truth, the highest good, which is the ultimate goal of all the world religions.

'Our duty as Christians is to place ourselves between two irreconcilable enemies. It remains to be seen which will win: the spirit of selfishness or the spirit of sacrifice.'

Frederic Ozanam, 1836

4. All the major religions believe that, ultimately, God is love.

5. The way of people to God is universally the way of sacrifice. The path of salvation everywhere begins with renunciation, the *via purgativa*. Repentance is the beginning of conversion and leads to contemplation and prayer. All the great saints of all high religions 'pray without ceasing'.
   As they advance they seek not earthly gods but God himself and God's rule on earth.

6. The great religions teach not only the way to God but always, at the same time, the way to the neighbour as well. All preach that the *via humana* is brotherly love, a love without limitations, extended even to enemies.

7. Finally, all of these religions accept that while religious experience is manifold and various, the superior way to God is love.

Conclusion

So it is not just the 'Vincentian' who is living and struggling with spirituality. All people who try to love God and each other are as well.

As we have been looking at people's relationships with God through history, we realise that we all are part of the great human mosaic of worship and service which is spirituality. Amidst the great changes in the Ireland of today, members of the svp face the huge challenge of giving meaning to their Christianity and of living their faith and values in the everyday reality. In doing this, they have a great Vincentian model, Frederic Ozanam, to guide them.

CHAPTER 5

A sense of Ireland

In this chapter I am writing about the 'external environment' of the svp – Ireland, its influences and its story or history. By taking a deeper look, not just at the present but at the past, the svp may come up with a different model of development for the future.

This Ireland of today, with its problems and potentialities, is the product of the choices people make today, but it is also, in a huge way, the product of its past history. If we want to understand the Ireland of today, if we are really to understand its spirit, its soul, its inner being, then we must reflect on its past. We must reflect on its childhood and adolescence if we are to understand its adulthood.

Stepping stones to the future

We are who we are today, for better or for worse. But we are who we are, because of where we came from. For that reason, a deeper sense of Ireland and an understanding of its history are essential to getting the best out of the Irish people today. Furthermore, this historical perspective will unveil some of Ireland's key characteristics or qualities, which I believe can be essential stepping stones to the future and the third millennium.

If the svp is to demand a deeper and more challenging response from the people of Ireland, including its own members, then the svp must look deeper, look longer, and look again (*re-spicere*, the meaning of the word respect). Frederic Ozanam would encourage this. The svp as an organisation has put much emphasis on Frederic Ozanam's call to action, 'It's action I want, not words', with little emphasis on the other side of his personality, the reflective and analytical side. Emphasis on one side without the other is a travesty of who

Frederic Ozanam was. His greatness was surely in the power and energy that came out of the pull of the two poles of his personality – reflection and action, philosophy and pragmatism.

I particularly emphasise Frederic Ozanam's qualities as philosopher and historian, and as analyst of the macro forces – historical, philosophical, economic, spiritual and social – which formed society, and continue to do so today, because all of this informed and enriched his life and work. It would do the same for the work of the svp in Ireland today. He would be encouraging the svp to look differently and deeper and so identify major stepping stones for the future.

He would have noted that the svp in Ireland in recent years has moved from dealing with the effects of poverty to looking at its causes, but he would be saying: 'Stand back further and see that there are other components, and other ways of looking besides just a socio-economic analysis. That surely is only one element of the jig-saw. What about an historical analysis, a theological and spiritual analysis as well as a social analysis?'

The story of Ireland

The story of Ireland is a wonderful story. It is a story of myth and magic, of triumphs and tragedies, of mist and mystery, of voyages and missions, of battles and of wars, a story of saints and scholars, of music and dancing, of spirits and spirituality. And it goes back a long way. The story of Ireland is a wonderful story of an island people, independent, inventive, resourceful, combative, intelligent, spiritual. It's a story of light and dark.

We, the Irish, are a melting pot of races and cultures that intermingled and produced what we are today. The first settlers (hunters) came from Scotland in the Stone Age, (8,000 BC); the second settlers (farmers) came from the Middle East, France and Spain at the end of the Stone Age, (3,000 BC); the Celts came from the Balkans and across Europe in the Iron Age, (600 BC); Patrick and Christianity came a little later (400 AD); the Vikings came around 800 AD, and the Normans came not long afterwards around 1,200 AD. All contributed to making us what we are today.

Part of Europe

Up to 12,000 BC, Ireland, like the rest of northern Europe, was still in the grip of the Ice Age. It was also joined physically to Britain and the Continent. About 10,000 BC, the southern tip of Ireland, from Wexford to Tralee, began to emerge from the ice. That probably explains how Kerry is the only county to win more than twenty-five All Irelands! About 9,000 BC, the ice had retreated, the seas rose and Ireland became an island. The retreating ice left many glacial valleys and mountains and islands, like Glendalough, Clew Bay, Blessington Lakes, the Gap of Dunloe, the mountains of Connemara.

An independent island people

The first settlers in Ireland were hunters. They came from Scotland to the northern part of the country. There are signs of them at Mount Sandal in Derry near the River Bann, and even down as far as Carlow. These were hunters-gatherers who lived on the rivers, lakes and sea shores and ate berries, fish, fowl, wild boar and red deer. These nomadic hunters have left their debris, especially remains of shellfish, on beaches from Dunquin in Kerry to Horn beach in Donegal, and under Ballybunion and Ballyconneely golf courses as well as at Lough Gara and Lough Corrib in Connacht.

So our first ancestors on the island of Ireland were hunters, adventurers, pathfinders. As an island people, they would have a separate identity and be independent of mind and spirit. This quality of independence of mind and spirit, which our first forebears passed on to us, has stood the Irish in good stead through the ages. It is the first stepping stone on which our future can be built.

If we want to understand the Ireland of today, if we
are to really understand its spirit, its soul, its inner
being, then we must reflect on its past. We must reflect
on its childhood and adolescence if we
are to understand its adulthood.

Second settlers

The first detailed knowledge we have of our ancestors and their qualities came with the arrival of the new Stone Age (Neolithic) people around 3,000 BC. They were farmers, the first farmers in Ireland and the forerunners of the IFA and Macra na Feirme! They came from the west of France and Spain, and before that from the Middle East. Some of these first farmers or their relatives had come from what is known as the Cradle of Civilisation on the Nile in Egypt and the Tigris and the Euphrates in Mesopotamia or Iraq. It was here on the banks of these rivers that, for the first time, because of the combination of rich soil, the sun, and water, enough food was produced to feed thousands of people. For the first time, all of the men didn't have to be hunters. This was one of the most important steps in the development of the human race. It was also the first unemployment crisis and the first time that the question of 'leisure-time' came up! But, of course, it had many positive values. It now allowed people time to develop other skills. Over the next 1,000 years, farmers, bronze-smiths, boat-builders, masons, priests, traders, crafts people developed.

From the Cradle of Civilisation to Ireland

When in 3,000 BC the first farmers came to Ireland in small boats and landed in Killala Bay and other ports in the west of Ireland, they would have brought all their stone tools and craft skills, their 'tamed' animals, and all their seeds for planting. 5,000 years later we have striking evidence of these people's way of life, at the Céide fields in Mayo and in the Boyne Valley especially.

The second settlers provided the second stepping stone on which Ireland has been built – wonderful skills in farming, craft and industry and creativity. Those skills are inherent in the Irish race and in every section of it, rich and poor.

The Celts

About 600 BC, the Celts came to Ireland from central Europe. They came in three waves. The Ereni came in 600 BC (Éire comes from them), the second called the Laighlin (a spear) came in 300 BC, and the third wave came in 50 BC. They were called the Gael because of the language they spoke, Gaelic. The Celts were to be the major determinants of the direction and character of Ireland for the next thousand years or more. They and Christianity totally influenced the formative or 'adolescent' years of the country. What were their chief characteristics? Their strong kingship or tribal grouping or *muintearas* – a sense of community or extended family, was their major contribution to Ireland. That *muintearas,* clannishness or total loyalty to the group, is still evident in the Ireland of today. Their worship of their Gods was famous – Bolg, the sun God, hence the Fir Bolg; Conn, hence *muintir Chonn-achta;* Eoghan, hence *Tír Eoghain*, and their beliefs gave them a great sense of identity and togetherness.

The Celts provided the third pillar or stepping stone in the development of Ireland – a great sense of community and loyalty.

Patrick and Christianity

Of all influences in Ireland and the Irish people, from the Ice Age to the Stone Age and the Bronze and Iron Age to that of modern Ireland, the greatest was surely Christianity. 432 AD is a key date, and the name Patrick is a key name in Irish history.

From the conversion of the Irish kings at Tara to the setting up of famous monasteries at Clonmacnoise, Bangor, Glendalough, Clonard, Kells and 800 more before the end of the sixth century, to the great Diaspora of Irish monks to the continent of Europe, Patrick's influence has spread. That missionary spirit and generosity of Patrick and his followers has spread through the centuries to the great Irish twentieth-century missionary exodus to the rest of the known world, where Irish missionaries, religious and lay, have brought spirituality, literacy, education, hospitals, health care and a way of life celebrated every year worldwide on St Patrick's day.

Christianity built on the strengths of the Celtic Irish – their loyalty to

'God', or the gods, their sense of community and duty to each member of the *tuath* or clan, and their care of each other.

And so Patrick and his followers provide us with a key fourth stepping stone for development today and in the future, which is Christian spirituality. 'You shall love the Lord your God with all your heart and with all your soul and you shall love your neighbour as you love yourself.' This is probably the key stepping stone for the development of Ireland today as a peaceful, sharing, caring nation with justice as the cornerstone.

The Famine

A fifth major influence on the Ireland of today is the Famine. The Irish nation was brought to its knees by the great Famine. Half the nation died or emigrated and the other half was traumatised. Has it recovered yet? This nation has suffered greatly, through hardships of living, through much oppression from invaders, but most of all through the cruelty and devastation of the Famine, an event that could have been prevented.

The Famine provides us with a fifth stepping stone or quality which is part of the Irish 'corporate personality' — suffering. Because of having suffered themselves the Irish have a lot of compassion. They have become known as a 'caring nation' in many parts of the world because of their caring and support for suffering nations and races throughout the years. This quality of compassion for suffering nations has been embodied in, and highlighted by, President Mary Robinson in modern times. Because the Irish have so often been oppressed, and have endured so much suffering and conflict, perhaps the greatest wish of the Irish people today is for peace.

Five stepping stones to the future

So there we have it, five major stepping stones to our future. These are five positive qualities which are deeply ingrained in the Irish nation and which can, and must, be tapped for future development:

A resilient people with independence of mind and spirit.

A skilful, resourceful, creative people.

A people with a strong sense of community and loyalty to each other.

A spiritual people with a mission to God and to each other.

A people who have suffered.

Five great ingredients for building a better future!

CHAPTER 6

Where from here?

'When you are up to your neck in crocodiles it is very hard to remember that your first intention was to drain the swamp!'

In this chapter we will look at the SVP in the Ireland of today. What are its concerns and priorities? Where is it going? We will start with some comments from the coalface:

'I enjoy the work of the Society. It is very challenging. It's not an à la carte menu you are coming to. If you say 'Yes' to Christ once, it's forever.'

'The SVP needs younger members. We are set in our ways. We are getting older.' 'Is the SVP creating dependency? We often feel it is. If we give money, the second and third generation will be dependent. If we don't, maybe the kids will go hungry. It's a no-win situation.'

'Maybe it's not either/or but both/and. Not either charity or justice but both charity and justice.'

These quotes, and others later on, from members of the SVP working at the coalface, show the range of issues, anxieties, struggles, questions, facing members working in Irish society today as we approach the end of the second millennium.

'There will always be tension at the coalface and in life. That must be part of Vincentian spirituality. It's the way of the cross, the way of love.'

'The SVP has got a bad image among young people. They see it for old men and women. We would have thought the same until we joined up and saw otherwise.'

'There is a danger that Central Office will have plans and strategies and neglect listening.'

'All we're doing is firefighting. It's sad to see a family being supported over time but not making it. That should not be happening in Ireland.'

The svp, like any other large organisation, is made up of all types of people, of all ages, with all types of personalities and backgrounds, and with different spiritualities and motivations and visions for the organisation. The common thread is that they are all 'value-driven' people working with and for the poor. None of them would say they are perfect but they are all trying to alleviate the effects of poverty, and where possible to minimise or eliminate the poverty. Setting corporate goals will therefore be a major concern for the svp now and in the future.

'I went to Sunshine House as a kid. I was so impressed by the patience and caring of the brothers, I said when I grow up I must say thanks by becoming a member too.'

'Ireland is the 26th richest country in the world and yet there is an awful lot of underdevelopment in Ireland. That shouldn't be. The svp must speak up more.'

'I'm unemployed among 75% unemployed in the area. I'm glad I'm unemployed as a conference member. I had to be depressed myself before I could understand how others are depressed. There's no reality until you have experienced that reality yourself.'

'We are living the life that Frederic Ozanam did with the poor. We are doing the work he did.'

'Well thought of organisation; rather timid however in confronting issues; can be ignored with impunity ... won't rock the proverbial boat.'

Prioritising, harnessing the present skills in the organisation in a more focused way, getting new blood, new members with new skills into the organisation; deepening and renewing and broadening the spirituality of the members; restructuring the organisation to minimise spillage of energy and maximise efficiency: these are some of the key svp issues which will decide its future in Ireland.

New era – new challenges

What is clear from listening to the svp members, and reading svp literature, is that they are all grappling with a new reality – the Ireland of today, a new era, changing times, changing values, changing perceptions and expectations, old issues in new guises. As Pope John Paul said, every new era and every new generation is a new continent, and new continents need to be explored, traversed, understood, and cultivated. As Ireland rose physically from under the ice in 10,000 BC, so a new Ireland has arisen today. It is no longer the isolated, rural, predominately Catholic island, hidden off the coast of mainland Europe. It is now the modern, industrialised, highly educated, sophisticated, pluralistic society, a member state of the European Union and a valued and dynamic member of the global village. The new Ireland has surfaced, with all the changes that reality brings.

That's the Ireland in which the SVP must operate today – the Ireland of the internet and the mobile phone, the Ireland of global TV and the global village, the Ireland of the consumer society meeting up with and challenging the caring Ireland and the Christian Ireland. It is estimated that more change has taken place in Ireland in the past fifty years than in the previous five hundred, except for the Famine.

Frederic Ozanam and change

Frederic Ozanam all his life was wrestling with change and was indeed very comfortable with change. Though he always had the long term view, he also saw the need to work in the short term, and to change with the needs of the times. This was his message to the Archbishop of Paris when looking for preaching in the modern form and in the arena of daily controversy. The very title of the newspaper which he helped to found, *New Era*, tells us that he wanted Catholics to look to the present and the future. Most of us are rearview mirror drivers through life, reacting to others and fearing how others might react, but Frederic Ozanam was never a prisoner of the rear-view mirror. He always kept his eyes on the road ahead! He too must have had his fears, and he certainly had his detractors, but neither dictated how he acted. The will of God and the needs of the poor were his sole criteria. That is why he was great. 'Feel the fear and do it' is a motto he would have approved of, and recommended to the SVP in Ireland today.

For God
is pleased
to bless
the tiny and
inconspicuous,
the mighty
tree in a
little seed.

Frederic Ozanam

It must be remembered that Frederic had to deal with a lot of difficult issues in his own life, so it wasn't easy. We often forget that our heroes and heroines in life are human too. When Frederic's mother died early in 1840 he was very upset and became very unsettled in his life and undecided about his future. He talked for long hours with his friend Lacondaire about joining a religious order, maybe the Dominicans. However, his old teacher and spiritual guide, Abbé Noirot, felt he hadn't got a vocation to the religious life, but that his vocation was as a lay person in the world. Frederic took this advice. That was a difficult time for Frederic, but he also had his consolations and supports.

In the following year, on 23 June 1841, Frederic married Amelie Soulacroix, a daughter of the Rector of the Lyons Academy, and four years later she gave birth to a daughter, whom they christened Marie. Frederic and Amelie doted on their daughter, who was their only child. Another Vincentian, François Lallier was her godfather. He was a great friend to the family and also a quiet support for Frederic.

Proud of SVP Ireland

If Frederic Ozanam were in Ireland today he would be very proud of the National Council of the SVP for attempting to redefine, reform and restructure the organisation in Ireland in order to move with the needs of the 'new era'. He would be equally proud of the Policy and Strategy Committee for helping it set priorities. He would be glad that they had a consultation of the members of the organisation rather than looking into their own hearts for the answers.

He would also be very much aware that there is a huge gap between policy and implementation, but he would be saying, 'Remember my words: it's action I want, not words!' And also, 'For God is pleased to bless the tiny and inconspicuous, the mighty tree in the little seed.' Plant the little seeds and they will grow.

He would be equally proud of the range of services of the Society, reflecting the fact that 'no work of charity is foreign to the Society' and, indeed, he would be especially proud of the contribution that women have made to the Society since 1967.

But he would also be saying: 'Ireland and our little organisation are at the crossroads. Look carefully, look back over the roads of history and spirituality from which both our organisation and Ireland have come. See the deep spirituality of Ireland – the Celts, Patrick, Brigid, Columbanus and all the missionaries – the faith of our fathers and mothers, the 'stories in stone' dotted across the Irish landscape – tombs, monasteries, crosses, chapels, Massrocks – see the suffering, see the faithfulness, see the resilience. What a great and deep story! What a great heritage! That heritage is still there deep in the Irish soul, the Irish psyche. It is written in their hearts, their souls, their blood, their collective memory, the marrow of their bones, their DNA. They cannot get rid of their spirituality and resilience and caring any more than they can get rid of their fighting temperament or culture or music. So look long and deep and help the young people of Ireland to find new ways to express their ideals and spirituality. You must challenge the Irish people more.'

svp at the crossroads

The way of the future of the svp as envisaged by the present leadership is contained in a very slim but very rich booklet called *Developing a Renewed Mission for the Society of St Vincent de Paul*, or the Mission Statement (1994).

Noel Clear, National President, says:

'In my address to the National Council in Killarney in June 1996, I made a commitment that for the next year, at all levels in the Society, we must concentrate on implementing in full the new Mission Statement of the Society.

It is a significant statement of what should be the thrust of the Society's work in Ireland in the years to come. Although it reflects a vision for the future, it bears an obvious resemblance to the spirit and thrust of the Rule of the Society in Ireland. It also is symbolic of the focus our founders had, more than one hundred and fifty years ago' (*The Bulletin*, Summer, 1996).

The President then outlined the central themes of the organisation's work: the Christian dimension, support and friendship, promoting self-sufficiency, and working for social justice.

He goes on: 'Inspired by our principal founder, Frederic Ozanam, and our patron, St Vincent de Paul, we seek to respond to the call every Christian receives to bring the love of Christ to those we serve in the spirit of the gospel message, "I was hungry and you gave me to eat"' (ibid).

Mission Statement

To celebrate the 150th anniversary of the foundation of the SVP in 1994, the Council of Ireland instructed the Policy and Strategy Committee to prepare a Mission Statement. 'This has to reflect the current role of the organisation and, in particular, the views of the members, in order that we undertake a reappraisal of the SVP's role in modern Ireland' (*Developing a Renewed Mission*, 1994:2).

Dr Paul Mooney and Associates, who did the research, set out their stall by stating that Mission Statements answer three key organisational questions:

(1) What is our purpose, why do we exist?

(2) What unique or distinctive competence do we have?

(3) What particular franchise or niche will we concentrate on?

Their questionnaire to the members then consisted of six questions:

(1) What are the key requirements of the people we serve?

(2) What are our current strengths as an organisation?

(3) Where are our current weaknesses as an organisation?

(4) Are there areas where we are not currently involved but should be?

(5) How important is the spiritual dimension to the work of the Society?

(6) What is our fundamental purpose as an organisation?

This questionnaire about needs, the organisation, the membership,

Mission Statement

The Society of St Vincent de Paul is a Christian lay voluntary organisation, working with the poor and disadvantaged. Inspired by our principal founder, Frederic Ozanam, and our patron, St Vincent de Paul, we seek to respond to the call every Christian receives to bring the love of Christ to those we serve in the spirit of the gospel message: 'I was hungry and you gave me to eat ...' (Mt 25).

No work of charity is foreign to the Society. We are involved in a diverse range of activities characterised by:

Support & friendship: Through person to person contact, we are committed to respecting the dignity of those we assist and thus to fostering their self-respect. In the provision of material and other support, we assure confidentiality at all times and endeavour to establish relationships based on trust and friendship.

Promoting self-sufficiency: We believe it is not enough to provide short-term material support. Those we serve must also be helped to achieve self-sufficiency in the longer term and the sense of self-worth this provides. When the problems we encounter are beyond our competence, we build bridges of support with others more specialised.

Working for social justice: We are committed to identifying the root causes of poverty and social injustice in Ireland and, in solidarity with the poor and disadvantaged, to advocate and work for the changes required to create a more just and caring society.

spirituality and the role or purpose of the Society, obviously threw up a lot of useful information.

Research and renewal

Research can obviously assist renewal. Whilst it is not possible or necessary to include the major findings of the research in this book, it may be useful to include some key points and conclusions of the authors.

At the outset, the point was made by the authors (Mooney & Imbusch) that developing a renewed mission for an organisation means firstly reviewing the present mission, aims, priorities and direction of the organisation, and then consciously making choices in developing a new mission, and selecting priorities and direction.

Commenting on the answers to the key question, 'What is our fundamental purpose as a organisation?', the authors write: 'The emerging difficulty is the lack of consensus on the fundamental purpose of the SVP. To some extent the SVP is unique in its 'broad' approach, as the vast majority of charitable organisations confine their focus to one of a small number of related areas, e.g. Simon, Bernados' (ibid: 33). Lack of consensus about the fundamental purpose or 'mission' of an organisation can 'dissipate resources and leave an uncomfortable vacuum with ambiguity and endless debate about our purpose' (ibid: 8).

They make the further point that 'The Society of St Vincent de Paul has reached a crossroads in its development as an organisation. This document (with the research results) attempts to detail the strategic issues facing the organisation at this point. We have not sought to provide answers to the problems raised, but to create an environment in which discussion and debate can take place' (ibid: 7).

It is precisely because the National Council wanted the SVP to take stock of itself, to see where it was and where it was going, that it instructed the Policy and Strategy Committee to prepare a new Mission Statement. As we have already seen, the President has placed the results of the research for the Mission Statement, and the Mission Statement itself, at centre stage for the Society.

The results of the research, the issues and anomalies it brings up for the members and the National Council, and the issues it doesn't answer, will be material for discussion and debate within the organisation for many years. Without a doubt, the little 'Pink Book', which contains this research (1994), and the little 'Blue Book' with the new Mission Statement (1995), will be key factors in deciding the future direction of the SVP in Ireland.

Bill Murray, Breffni Regional President, rightly makes a strong plea for the material in the little 'Pink Book' to be the subject of dialogue and discussion in conferences. Quoting Pope John Paul's call for a new evangelism and missionary crusade in the face of an uncaring and materialistic world, Bill says: 'There are many challenges, not only for the church but also, I suggest, for the Society of St Vincent de Paul' (*The Bulletin*, summer 1997:5). Having located the mission of the SVP within the mission of the worldwide church, Bill says: 'The Society's Rule, the Members Handbook, and, probably the most important of all, the recently published Mission Statement, must be understood and appreciated by all' (ibid: 5). These would seem to be prophetic words.

The two Irelands

Whilst there is obviously much soul searching going on within the organisation about its life, its spirit, its structure, recruitment roles and goals, the SVP continues to pursue its dual mandate of (i) being with the marginalised and of (ii) fighting for social justice.

Basically, it does this work in three ways:
(1)   As an organisation in its own right:
         It works with the marginalised
         It speaks on behalf of the marginalised in its annual reports
      Its makes submissions to government
(2)   In partnership with others:
         Working at local community level

Working with statutory bodies
The Vincentian Partnership for Justice
Partnership in the National Anti-Poverty Strategy
Partnership with parishes in 32 counties
Working with the new Government Area Partnerships

(3) As a Network Convenor

The svp is a catalyst, or network convenor, in so far as it brings groups together around such issues as poverty, homelessness, domestic violence, drugs, unemployment. Members are also network convenors for poor areas and the marginalised in general in so far as they bring together, for policy makers and the public, the collective experience of the marginalised. They are network convenors in so far as they are an organisation and a focal point for the marginalised. The job of the svp, in this context, has been to unite diverse minorities around primary goals. This networking role also tries to focus public opinion in order to help the two Irelands to tolerate each other, to understand each other, and to work together for the good of all.

When the problems we encounter
are beyond our competence, we
must build bridges of support
with others more specialised.

Noel Clear

Where from here?

From even a short reflection on the literature and work of the SVP in Ireland, it is obvious that the way of the future of the SVP is a most challenging and most exciting one. Where it goes from here will depend on the leadership, the attitudes of the members, the changing needs, and many more 'x' factors. What is clear is that the SVP must see itself as less of a 'petrol-pump' or service type of organisation, and more of a 'partnership-in-development' organisation working in solidarity with the marginalised.

As Noel Clear says: 'We believe it is not enough to provide short-term material support (today). Those we serve must also be helped to achieve self-sufficiency in the longer term and the sense of self-worth this provides. When the problems we encounter are beyond our competence, we must build bridges of support with others more specialised' (*The Bulletin*, Summer 1997:3).

The President also gives a clear pointer to the future when he says: 'The challenge, as we move into the new millennium, is for the Society to network with many other services which are impacting on the lives of the people we serve, and to influence the development of local communities. Promoting 'self-sufficiency' is a theme we must keep on the agenda of all our Councils and Conferences if we are really to make a difference to the lives of even a small number of the families we serve' (ibid:4).

One gets a strong sense of healthy questioning at all levels of the SVP in Ireland today. This can only be good and augurs well for the future.

Two models

The SVP in Ireland has to be inspired by its two great models, St Vincent de Paul its patron, and Frederic Ozanam its founder. Two great prophets and pragmatics! Listen to Frederic's words about the person he and his young idealistic friends chose as patron. 'Vincent de Paul was not the man to build on sand or for the moment. The great souls who draw nigh unto God have something of the gift of prophecy. Let us not hesitate to believe that St Vincent had a vision of the evils and the needs of our times. He is still making a provision. Like all great founders he never ceases to have his spiritual posterity alive and active amid the ruins of the past. In our patron we shall honour a father. Who knows but that one day we shall see the children of our old age shelter in the bosom of a wide spreading Society over whose birth we have watched.'

In Frederic Ozanam, their founder, the Irish 'Vincentians' have a model of tireless giving of self to God and the poor.

All his life, because of his giftedness, his ability to communicate the deepest thoughts in the language and idiom of the everyday, and his attractive and lively personality, Frederic was hugely in demand. Public speeches, academic lectures, debates with working men's groups, writing articles for newspapers and journals, all took up his time. All of this was over and above his university lectures and tutorials, his writing of books, and most importantly, his care of his family. Frederic's constant demands on himself finally undermined his health which was never over robust. Even after his health broke down completely in 1848, Frederic continued to visit conferences all over France, England and Italy. It was while returning from Vienna, where he tried to set up a conference, that Frederic Ozanam died at Marseilles on 18 September 1853, the feast of Our Lady's birth. He died as he lived, in the presence of God and doing God's work.

CHAPTER 7

Millennium challenge

'I ask you: let us occupy ourselves with people who have too many needs and not enough rights, who call out rightly for a greater involvement in public affairs, for guarantees of work — and who cry out against misery.'— Frederic Ozanam, 1848

From the author's reflection on the life of Frederic Ozanam, on the SVP in Ireland, and on the Ireland of today, six challenges seem to have emerged for the SVP at the start of the third millennium:

1. Ozanam's Christian social teaching.
2. The challenge of the millennium itself.
3. Putting poverty at the top of the national agenda.
4. SVP and young people.
5. Violence against women: A men's issue.
6. A spirituality for the third millennium

1. Ozanam's Christian social teaching

A major challenge for the SVP in Ireland as we approach the third millennium is to reclaim and proclaim the Christian social teaching of its founder.

In 1848, when Frederic Ozanam wrote the above words, he was coming to the end of his short life. Five years later he would be dead at forty, having given his life to the spread of the gospel and the service of the poor. He, like the patron of the Society, St Vincent de Paul, made an 'option for the poor' when that term wasn't known. For twenty years Frederic had studied, reflected, written, lectured, and campaigned for a just society in France. This was a society based on the values of the gospel of Jesus and the principles of liberty, equality and fraternity. Till his death, Frederic never ceased to work at the macro level, through any avenue possible, enunciating principles and policies for social cohesion, the rights and responsibilities of property, worker education, Trade Unions, and Christian democracy. He also ran classes on these topics with other members of the svp. This man was truly ahead of his time!

It is not surprising that the social encyclicals of Popes, from Pope Leo xiii's *Rerum Novarum* in 1891 to Pope John xxiii's *Pacem in Terris,* were re-stating and developing many of Ozanam's teachings. One example is Pope Leo's teaching on the just wage. Pope Leo wrote: 'To misuse men as though they were things in the pursuit of gain, or to value them solely for their physical power – that is truly shameful and inhuman.' Frederic Ozanam had written fifty years earlier: 'There is exploitation when the master considers the worker not as an associate, as a helper, but as an instrument, from which he must draw maximum service at the lowest possible cost.'

There is no doubt that Ozanam's Christian social teaching, together with the social encyclicals of the Popes, which are an elaboration and development of it, would be of great benefit to the Society's work and to the Ireland of today. The Vincentian Partnership for Justice (Daughters of Charity, Vincentian Order, svp) has made a very interesting and valuable excursion into this area through its Voter Education Programme. The svp, the Vincentian Partnership for Justice, and bodies like cori (Conference of Religious of Ireland), can make a difference in the area of national social policy and national education for democracy because they are seen to be politically independent and because their teachings are based on the bedrock of Christianity.

Though he was dogged with ill health for much of his later life, Frederic nevertheless gave his total energy to applying the gospel to society, and to his work among the poor. Frederic's practical work among the poor gave him great insight into the plight of the working class and it also gave him credibility to speak with authority on the major issues of a society that had been

The key to the future is having and building caring local communities.

Bill Cleary

devastated and divided by the Revolution. The SVP can speak and act from the same position of strength in Ireland.

2. The challenge of the millennium

The second major challenge for the SVP is the millennium itself. The millennium, celebrated once every thousand years, is obviously a very special time. The millennium is a time of celebration, a time of change, a time to look back and a time to look forward. It is also a time of reflection and renewal. 'The millennium is like a huge magnet or moral force on humanity, amplifying emotions, heightening awareness, accelerating change, and compelling people to examine themselves, their values and their organisations' (Naisbitt and Aburdene, 1990:1).

In biblical and Christian terms, the millennium has extra special meaning. Firstly, it is celebrating two thousand years of Christianity. As Pope John Paul II says in his Apostolic Letter, *Tertio Millennio Adveniente*, 'The year 2000 invites us to gather with renewed fidelity and ever deeper communion along the banks of this great river: The River of Revelation, and of Christianity, a river which flows through human history starting from the event which took place at Nazareth and then at Bethlehem 2000 years ago' (25). Secondly, the year 2000 is a jubilee, and 'jubilee' has huge significance in biblical terms. In the Old Testament, a 'jubilee' year occurred every seven years and debts were pardoned (Deuteronomy 15:1-2). Every fifty years was a 'special jubilee' or 'year of the Lord's favour', when debts were forgiven, slaves were set free, and communities set aside hostilities and divisions (Leviticus 25:8-10). The greatest 'jubilee' or 'year of the Lord's favour' was the coming of Jesus himself. He said that, when he read in the Temple from Isaiah, 'He has sent me to bring good news to the poor, to proclaim liberty to captives, to set the down-trodden free and to proclaim the year of the Lord's favour' (Luke 4:16-21).

What wonderful words! If we Christians only understood them! Pope John Paul says: 'While I invite the lay faithful to pray to the Lord for the light and assistance necessary for the preparation and celebration of the forthcoming jubilee, I exhort ecclesial communities to open their hearts to the prompting of the Spirit. He will not fail to arouse enthusiasm and lead people to celebrate the jubilee with renewed faith and generous action' (59).

The svp and the millennium

What are the promptings of the Spirit to the svp? Is the svp ready to take up the challenge of the millennium itself? Has it got the imagination, the courage, and the trust in God? Has it got the leadership, the policies, the structures and the personnel? Will it respond to the challenges of its principal founder, Frederic Ozanam, who continuously pushed his co-founders to fight their comfortable status quo mentality? Remember his continuous 'afflicting the comfortable' within society, the Catholic Church and the rich in France. Frederic was a prophet, not a pleaser, and the prophet will always afflict the comfortable, including himself or herself, in order to comfort the afflicted. The major question is: 'Is the svp coping with the major social, economic, moral and spiritual changes that are occurring in Ireland at the end of the twentieth century? Is it able to make some of the deep and radical changes that are necessary? Many businesses have made these changes. Some haven't and have disappeared. Some religious orders have made deep changes. Others haven't and will disappear. The churches are having major difficulties with change. Every Christian organisation is called to continuous and radical change. It is always being called to die to its old self in order to be born anew, like the caterpillar into the butterfly.

3. Eradication of poverty

A third major millennium challenge for the svp is continuing its ongoing battle against poverty in Ireland. Perhaps the most realistic and worthwhile target for the svp would be to get the elimination of poverty to the top of the national political agenda for the start of the third millennium.

Every Christian organisation
is called to continuous and
radical change. It is
always being called
to die to its old
self in order to
be born anew,
like the
caterpillar
into the
butterfly.

As the report on the consultation document of the churches in Northern Ireland, *Poverty and Social Exclusion in the EU*, says: 'The primary responsibility for addressing poverty and social exclusion must rest with the statutory authorities' (Belfast 1996:4). However, voluntary bodies like the SVP have an important role to play. Being the 26th richest nation in the world, having such a small population – less than five million on the whole island – having so many resources on land and sea, and having such an educated and talented workforce, is there any excuse for such poverty in Ireland? The poverty blackspots, so prevalent in both urban and rural areas, are a blot on the face of the island of Ireland.

The Celtic Tiger and poverty

Time magazine, *The Economist* and *Der Spiegel*, the German news magazine, all have been writing recently in admiration of Ireland's booming economy, using accolades like 'The Celtic Tiger', 'Europe's Shining Light', and 'the prosperous green island that was Europe's poor house for generations'. All these accolades are deserved because they reflect the reality of Ireland today. Just recently Ireland has been declared the 16th most competitive country in the world's economic order, moving close to the top of the world's premier league, behind Singapore, Hong Kong and the USA (*World Economic Forum*, 1997). The prosperity of Ireland at the moment, and the fact that the rising tide is not raising the boats of the less well-off, is causing much debate in the national media.

The national debate

Here is a sample of different comments and views expressed in the public forum about poverty and economic prosperity:

'Evidence suggests that Northern Ireland is the poorest region in the UK. 38% of households live in poverty.'

Northern Ireland Anti-Poverty Network (NIAPN) 1996

'Although Northern Ireland is the poorest region within the whole UK, conflict and division have meant that effective debate on poverty issues has to a large extent been marginalised.'

Northern Ireland Anti-Poverty Network (NIAPN), 1996

'Smurfit warns against creation of two-tier society in Ireland.'

Irish Times, April 1997

'The Celtic Tiger is like the cuckoo for the marginalised, heard in the distance but never seen in one's own neighbourhood.'

Bishop Brendan Comisky, Pastoral Letter, 2 June 1997

'There is something badly wrong with the Celtic Tiger. There are more people with incomes below the poverty line in Ireland today than there were a decade ago, 34 per cent compared to 30 per cent.'

Sean Healy, Conference of Religious of Ireland (CORI), *Irish Times*, 3 June 1997

'People want to see that government has the right balance between free-market principles and social concern.'

John Bruton, Taoiseach, June 1997

'Zero tolerance for crime is meaningless unless there is similar intolerance for the greater crime of poverty in a time of unprecedented national growth.'

Bishop Brendan Comisky, 2 June 1997

'Many members will tell you that they have been involved with some families for two or three generations. These families have been caught in the poverty trap.'

Noel Clear, President (*The Bulletin*, Summer 1997:3)

As the nurturers and carers, women have borne a
major burden of looking after the needs of the
family and children.

The SVP challenge

The SVP has contributed much to this debate on poverty in both parts of Ireland over the past twenty years. In common with other anti-poverty organisations, their understanding of the issue has deepened and their demand for the elimination of the two-tier society has got stronger. Most importantly also, the SVP in the thirty-two counties has itself begun to develop models of education, self-help and development in solidarity with the marginalised, and in partnership with other voluntary and statutory bodies, which is itself part of the answer to the problem of poverty. This is a most healthy development and would delight Frederic Ozanam who believed so much in education, fraternity or solidarity, and democracy in action.

It would seem that a new milestone has been reached in the Republic of Ireland with the publication of the Government National Anti-Poverty Strategy, *Sharing in Progress* (1997). The SVP made a very valuable contribution to this document with many other voluntary agencies. Its task now is to keep the contents of this document to the forefront of national policy making as we approach the millennium. In fact, the SVP, north and south, must continue to be the voice for the voiceless, while at the same time enabling people and communities to speak for themselves, as in the Voter Education Programme.

4. Millennium challenge for young people

At its first beginnings, the SVP was a society set up by young people, and run by young people in the service of the poor. When it began in Ireland in the 1840s, it was equally a young people's organisation. This did not preclude adults but its driving force in Paris as in Dublin was the zeal, enthusiasm, radicalism and commitment of youth. It must not be forgotten either that the setting up of SVP was part of the twin-track approach of Frederic Ozanam, to give young people a living committed faith and spirituality, and to have them express that faith in action for the poor. So both Frederic Ozanam's articula-

A RIVER OF LOVE

tion and proclamation of Christianity, and his development of the work of justice among the poor, were youth-centred enterprises.

Where have all the youth gone? Perhaps it is time for the SVP to reflect again on the mission and charisma of its principal founder, especially regarding young people. Is there a better time to challenge the youth of Ireland with the values of the gospel and the radicalism of justice? At a time of much disillusionment with large impersonal institutions and bureaucracies, at a time of apathy with politics and politicians, at a time of massive change, perhaps it is time to challenge young people in a deeper way? Pope John Paul II did that when he proposed Frederic Ozanam as a model for the youth of the world. Should the SVP in Ireland do anything less with the youth of Ireland?

So, a fourth millennium challenge for the SVP is to review its relationships with youth and to challenge them in the light of its principal founder's vision and affirmation for young people. This challenge should include the possible role of a lay Christian organisation in the development and formation of young people, in view of the decline of religious and clergy. Perhaps an integrated spiritual-plus-action-for-justice model would reflect Frederic Ozanam's dual approach mentioned above?

The greatest challenge for the SVP concerning youth, or returning to a 'youth-driven organisation', is the challenge of imagination. It is more a challenge for artists and seers, for youth and for prophets and dreamers like Frederic Ozanam, than for just any committee made up of adults, especially adults who may have given up on the youth of today!

5. Women's issues: Violence against women

Since Frederic Ozanam and his young friends were first inspired by a woman, Sr Rosalie, in the slums of Paris, the SVP has been supporting women in bringing up their families, often in grinding poverty. As the nurturers and carers, women have borne a major burden of looking after the needs of the family and children. Over the years, the SVP has continued to support women in this often difficult task and also provided home management, education and development programmes for them. The SVP is no stranger to the suffering of women, especially when continuous unemployment, poverty, crime or drugs hit their neighbourhood or their family.

Violence against women: A men's issue

But of all the suffering of women, one of the most sad and most serious is violence against women. And violence against women is a men's issue, because men are the perpetrators. It is more appropriate and just that the brothers of the perpetrators, rather than the sisters of victims, do something about violence against women. The SVP could make a serious contribution if it became a catalyst with other voluntary organisations for a movement of men to campaign against this violence against women.

Just recently, CORI, the Conference of Religious in Ireland, has produced a document on violence against women, *Where Home is Where the Hurt is* (1997). It is intended as a resource for churches in tackling the problem of the abuse of women. In supporting this initiative, Sean Brady, Archbishop of Armagh, says: 'We live in a culture of violence. Domestic violence is now a serious social evil ... We must all try to build a future that is free from violence. Tackling violent relationships and the root causes of them is a good way to start' (*Irish Times*, 18 June 1977).

The Task Force Report on Violence against Women, launched in May 1997, concluded with two important points: (1) that women are most at risk from known men, that the abuse is widespread, occurs in all social classes, and that the increase in this violence requires a national strategy; (2) that there must be a total acceptance that violence against women is wrong, that it is a criminal offence, and that there is no acceptable level of violence.

Men of violence

The term 'men of violence' is the one usually associated with paramilitary organisations. But there is another category of 'men of violence' in Ireland — those who beat their wives or partners in their homes. Sometimes these men are alcoholics or violent men outside the home, but often they are seen as kind, caring men in the community, but are vicious, brutal people in the home.

Why does there seem to be so much violence in the male of the species? Most vandalism, violent crime, break-ins, robberies, assaults, punishment beatings, killings, are done by men. Why? Man the hunter, the macho male, alien to the field of feelings, without a language to express the inner world, has to come to terms with the darkside of his male world. To acknowledge the reality is the start of a cure. To try to understand the causes is the second step.

To do something about it is the third. Maybe for the millennium, men in our Society will take up the cause of violence against women. The svp can help them to do so.

6. A spirituality for the third millennium

The story of Irish spirituality is written as a story in stone right across the face of Ireland. This story in stone is the outward enduring sign of a 5000-year story of the soul of the Irish people. It is the story of their relationships with their Gods at first, and then with their God, and also the story of the lived expressions of those relationships. It is a story that begins in the Stone Age with the large passage graves at Newgrange, Knowth and Dowth in the Boyne Valley (3,000 BC). The story of Stone Age spirituality is also visible at the Céide fields in Mayo and is expressed in the dolmens in the Burren and dotted right across the land. It is also a story of stone circles, which were places of ritual before churches were built and the forerunners of the headstones of today. The story of Irish spirituality is also a story of Celtic crosses and monasteries from Clonmacnoise to Armagh, from Glendalough to Louth Derg, from Tara to Achill Island. It is also a story of beehive huts to massrocks to holy mountains to modern churches. The latest chapter in the story in stone (or steel) is the large cross erected in the Phoenix Park in Dublin for Pope John Paul II's visit in 1979.

'While I invite the lay-faithful to pray to the Lord for the light and assistance necessary for the preparation and celebration of the forthcoming jubilee, I exhort ecclesical communities to open their hearts to the prompting of the Spirit. He will not fail to arouse enthusiasm and lead people to celebrate the jubilee with renewed faith and generous action.'

Pope John Paul II

5000-year story

This long story of the spirituality of the Irish is expressed, not just in stone but in art, in music, in poetry and literature, in Mass and rituals, in missions and pilgrimages, in orphanages, hospitals and night shelters. It is also expressed in honouring the dead, in celebrating life, rites of passage, love of neighbour, in the care of the sick, and the work of justice.

This 5,000-year story in stone is the enduring reminder of the depth of spirituality of the Irish people. It is a spirituality which has brought them through good times and bad times, through famine and oppression, through voyages and missions, through life and death. This story of the Irish spirit, or the spirit of the Irish, is long and deep and ingrained in the psyche and heart and bones of every Irish person. It is part of being Irish, just as politics and literature and drinking Guinness are.

A spirituality for the third millennium

Since the svp is above all a value-driven organisation, or a spiritually-driven organisation, it is important that it reflect on and clarify its spirituality for the third millennium. This is vitally important for a number of reasons:

(i)   to nurture and develop the spirituality of its members.
(ii) to have an organisational spirituality which will underpin, nourish and expand its development in the new millennium.
(iii) to have a spirituality for the 'new era' or the 'new continent' which is the Ireland of today.
(iv) to have a deep and rooted Christian lay spirituality.
(v)   to have a spirituality which will reflect the best of Vatican II, Celtic, biblical and Vincentian spiritualities.
(iv) to have, above all, a spirituality that reflects the life and work of its principal founder Frederic Ozanam.

This Ozanam spirituality was God-centred and life-centred, creation-centred and Christ-centred, personal and social.

It was mystical and prophetic, about worship and service.

It included a personal spirituality, a spirituality of service and of justice and a spirituality of society (Christian democracy).

Conclusion:

'The Christian hope is for all to be able some day to participate fully in the one family. Working towards a true community demands preferential treatment of the poor, one which strives to create opportunities for the deprived and oppressed so that all will be someday able to participate fully in the Body of Christ.'

Those words sound like Frederic Ozanam's but they are not his. They were written by Maura Mulhall, a Vincentian, in her reflection on the family of God, the Trinity and the SVP (Mulhall, 1995:45). But how they reflect Frederic's basic theme: 'We're all God's family. All things have him as their source. All relationships and actions must be based on his laws of love. Building a civilisation of love is the greatest good.'

'Inclusiveness' (treating everyone the same) or 'Fraternity' could be Frederic's second name. He gave his all to God, to the less well-off, to his family and friends. He was outstandingly gifted, of that there can be no doubt. He could have been self-opinionated and arrogant but he was a humble person and was supposed to have had a great sense of humour. By all accounts, he made a lot of jokes at his own expense and he also wrote humorous verse – probably in ten languages! He once wrote forty verses about a wrestling match!

There is one thing we can be certain of about Frederic Ozanam. He wasn't, or couldn't be, into creating monuments to himself. He had only one concern, to build a better, more humane and more fraternal world. And the blueprint for that could be found in the heart of God and the life and teaching of Christ.

What better way to end this short reflection on Frederic Ozanam than to quote from his final testimony or will? Here are his farewell words to his family, his wife Amelie, his daughter Marie, and members of SVP:

'I bid a farewell, short as the things of earth, to my dear Amelie, who has been the joy and charm of my life and whose tender care has softened all my pain for more than a year. I thank her, I bless her, I await her in heaven. There, and only there, can I give her such love as she deserves.

I give to my child the benediction of the Patriarchs, in the name of the Father and of the Son and of the Holy Ghost. I am sad that I cannot labour longer at the dear task of her education, but I entrust her absolutely to her virtuous and well-beloved mother.

I implore the prayers of my friends, of the Society of St Vincent de Paul. Let not your zeal be slackened by those who will say, he is in heaven. Pray unceasingly for one who loved you all much. Sure of your supplication, dear, kind friends, I shall leave this world with less fear. I firmly hope that we shall not be separated and that I shall remain in the midst of you until you rejoin me. May the blessing of God the Father, the Son and the Holy Ghost rest upon all of you. Amen.'

Bibliography

Casey, Michael, *What are we at? Ministry and Priesthood for the Third Millennium*, The Columba Press, Dublin 1992

Derum, James Patrick, *Apostle in a Top Hat*, SVP, St Louis Missouri 1995

Developing a Renewed Mission for the SVP, SVP, Dublin 1994 (1), 1995 (2)

Fagan, Austin, *Through the Eye of a Needle*, St Paul/Universe Publications, England 1989

Frederic Ozanam, SVP Booklet, Dublin 1961

Global Competitiveness Report, World Economic Forum, Switzerland 1997

Joyce, James, *A Portrait of the Artist as a Young Man*, Penguin Books, New York 1960

Martin, Gerry, *The Bulletin*, SVP, Dublin 1996

Mulhall, Maura, 'The Impact of a New Theology of Trinity on a lay organisation', unpublished thesis, Dublin 1995

Murphy, Michael, *The Frederic Ozanam Story*, SVP, Dublin 1977

Naisbitt, John & Aburdene, Patricia, *Megatrends 2000*, Sedgwick & Jackson, London 1990

Report on the Consultation Document of the Churches in Northern Ireland on Poverty and Exclusion in the EU, Belfast 1996

Report on Violence against Women, Government Publications, Dublin 1977

Sharing in Progress, National Anti-Poverty Strategy, Government Publications, Dublin 1997

The Northern Ireland Declaration on Poverty, Northern Ireland Anti-Poverty Network (NIAPN) 1996

The Vocation and Mission of the Lay Faithful, Christifideles Laici, Pope John Paul II, 1988

Vincentian Partnership for Justice, Ozanam House, Dublin 1997

When Home is where the hurt is, Conference of Religious of Ireland (CORI), 1997

Though he and others were in the business of planting acorns, he could always see the possibility of oak trees.